THE
SCIENCE OF
CREATING YOUR
HAPPINESS

SAHIL ANEJA

outskirtspress
DENVER, COLORADO

Outskirts Press, Inc.
http://www.outskirtspress.com

ISBN: 978-1-4787-2279-3

Outskirts Press and the "OP" logo are trademarks belonging to Outskirts Press, Inc.

PRINTED IN THE UNITED STATES OF AMERICA

GIFT TO: _____ *Drew* _____

FROM: _____ *Sahil* _____

I _____ choose to be
consistently happy and make others happy by utilizing
and constantly sharing the studies of *Happiology:
The Science of Creating Your Happiness.*

Happiness First!

The Wisdom of Youth

"A positive attitude is not a destination.
It is a way of life."
~*Linda McLean*

It is my great pleasure to introduce to you Mr. Sahil Aneja, author of *Happiology*. As a published author myself, I can attest to the journey of dedication that Sahil has completed to reach this point. Writing a book is no small feat. Becoming a published author is a dream often held by many, but achieved by the determined few.

Now, consider this: Sahil is an accomplished, published author in his own right, at the age of 17. The reality is, despite all the talent and potential that aspiring authors of all ages possess, not many 17 year olds possess the commitment and follow-through to finish a project of this magnitude.

This is only scratching the surface when it comes to Sahil's remarkable accomplishment. In the following pages, he takes on an extremely enlightened topic requiring a significant level of emotional and intellectual maturity. *Happiology* guides us on the path to understanding the importance of engaging the mind to live fully in the existence we each desire.

The layers uncovered on such a journey are not thin either. To fully engage one's mind means understanding all aspects of how the mind works as well as ways in which it can act as saboteur or soul mate. Once we have begun to grasp these concepts, we begin to peel back even more layers of the onion, exposing the truth behind our emotions, our beliefs, the agreements we have with ourselves that create the results we see in life and so much more.

One topic Sahil discusses that is also a personal passion of my own is the practice of gratitude. I'm impressed with how he discusses this subject with the wisdom of an "old soul."

There has been a significant amount of research done on the effects of gratitude. Dr. Robert Emmons (University of California Psychologist and Professor) found that practicing intentional gratitude permanently alters our level of happiness and positivity. His studies[1] concluded that "participants in a mindset of gratitude felt more joyful, enthusiastic, interested, attentive, energetic,

---

1   Emmons, Dr. Robert A. "thanks!" (Emmons & McCullough, 2003)

Gratitude creates positive thoughts and thinking positive thoughts creates positive actions, which leads to positive results.

Positive Thoughts -> Positive Actions -> Positive Results

Or as Sahil puts it – "From gratitude comes greatness."Before you turn the page and begin the special journey into Happiology that Sahil has mapped out, there are a few things I would like you to do. First, open your mind to all the possibilities that await you. Then, fill your heart with the spirit of gratitude, in anticipation of receiving this gift of knowledge. Now, I am pleased to introduce you to the words and message of a truly remarkable young author.

-Linda McLean, CEO and founder of McLean International, is an international, certified business and life coach, speaker, and the author of the #1 International bestselling book *Next Level Living – Today's Guide for Tomorrow's Abundant Life, My Gratitude Journal* and *Mind, Millions & Memories.* Her company offers the tools and knowledge gained from over 25 years of business, leadership and team development coaching/consulting to help individuals and businesses reach their next level of success in all areas of life. Visit her website, www.McleanInternational.com.

excited, determined and strong" These same participants were also more willing to offer others emotional support. Participants experiencing gratitude reported sleeping better, increased positive feelings, and increased life satisfaction. They were 25% happier overall than before they began this experiment.

Psychologist Glen Affleck also conducted a study that indicates those heart patients "who feel appreciative of life" after a heart attack have reduced risks for subsequent attacks.

These studies and others prove that having an "attitude of gratitude" can have very positive physical effects on one's life. How we feel about our lives matters. Being grateful, even for the smallest things, lowers our stress, prevents disease, can extend our lives, and causes us to experience more enjoyment. Expressing gratitude makes those around us feel good as well.

One of the best ways to circumvent negative reactions and thoughts is to focus on those things you are grateful for. Gratitude is one of the most positive emotions we can experience. If you spend a few moments each day, particularly in the morning, focusing on those things that you are grateful for, it blocks many of the negative emotions you may habitually struggle with. This is especially helpful at first when you are becoming aware of how much negativity there is in your life. Gratitude keeps you hopeful and allows you to move forward instead of staying mired in negative thoughts and emotions.

Why Happiness?

With a growingly depressed world, happiness is what basically everyone desires. Yet, so few have found their way to it. Since you have picked up *Happiology: The Science of Creating Your Happiness*, the time is now to begin transforming into a consistently happy person!

STOP making excuses!
STOP feeling sorry for yourself!
STOP living an unfulfilling life!
START being happy!
WATCH everything fall into place!
ENRICH your life with happiness!

Everyone wants it, yet very few attain it. You can be one of the lucky ones if you use this book with the following guidelines:

- Read every single chapter (not just one or two)
- Reread them multiple times
- Practice and use the Happiology methods and exercises
- Write in this book! Make it personal and make it yours!
- Share your happiness with others

Accept the terms of this challenge, and happiness will be yours!

My Special Thanks To:

My family—My grandparents, father, mother, sister, aunts, uncles, and cousins whose nonstop support, belief, help, motivation, and love has inspired me throughout this process. I cannot thank you enough.

My teachers, school staff, and friends—All those who, throughout my years of education, have helped me learn, grow, and develop as an individual with their wisdom and humor. Thank you.

To God—Who has blessed me with more than I could ever ask for and who has guided me through all walks of life. Thank You.

To authors and motivators—Such as Zig Ziglar, Dale Carnegie, T. Harv Eker, Joel Osteen, Will Smith, Linda

McLean, and many others who have motivated me to become better and do more. Thank you.

Lastly, to all those naysayers and nonbelievers—You all inspire me to do better. The challenge of proving that it can be done is a huge motivation in itself. Thank you.

P.S. If I forgot to mention you, please accept my thanks.

An Extra Thanks To:

My dad, Sanjeev Aneja. His inspiration throughout my entire life has guided me to the point where I could write this book and think the way I do. At age 8, it was he who introduced me to speaker T. Harv Eker at an engaging seminar, which immediately had me in love with business, goal setting, and success. Doing the things in that convention at such a young age purified my mindset and is an experience I cannot forget. I wasn't comfortable at first, and I did not want to do it, but with my dad's inspiration, I did, and it truly changed my life.

It was my dad who introduced me to and constantly played the voices of Zig Ziglar, Jim Rohn, Bob Proctor, and others to motivate me and get me thinking about happiness and success. Starting at a very young age, it was from his library that I was reading books like *Think and Grow Rich, The Power of Positive Thinking, How to*

Win Friends and Influence People, and *See You at the Top*.

And, of course, his leadership and inspiration by example has helped me learn and grow so much. His book *For It To Be It's Up To Me*, got me thinking about my own take on life and happiness. By seeing my father so dedicated to his business, clients, family, book, and God, I am always inspired to push myself farther and do more. Without his help, guidance, and love, none of this would be possible. Thank you so much.

—Sahil

The Studies of Happiology:

Are you ready to start **creating** your happiness?

How Do I Create My Happiness?

Genuine happiness, contrary to popular belief, is a science. It is a study, a skill, and a habit that takes proper practice and development to achieve. *Happiology: The Science of Creating Your Happiness,* if read thoroughly and with an open mind, has the power to make *any* individual going through *any* set of circumstances happy. You will learn that, regardless of your circumstances, you can achieve what people want most in life: Happiness.

As a 16-year-old who is said to be mature for his age, I have spent much of my life reading, analyzing, evaluating, and assessing how happy both I and the people around me are. After several observations and discoveries, I have found the essential roots of happiness that anyone (yes, anyone) can develop. Circumstances do not matter. All that matters is your desire, your commitment, and your attitude toward becoming a consistently happy individual. This book will guide you through these steps and will immediately have you on your way to becoming a happier individual!

Happy reading!

Happiness is Non-Circumstantial

As human beings, our emotions are fickle and extremely prone to changing on a regular basis. From happiness to sorrow, every day brings with it new feelings towards life. As a result, we crave consistency from life in order to maintain some stability. However, we refrain from recognizing why our lives are so emotionally unstable. The answer is simple, and the solution to living happily every day can be attained by following the path to joyfulness featured in *Happiology: The Science of Creating Your Happiness*.

The cause of emotional instability in our lives can be traced back to the roots of emotions: the events. Events, or things that happen in our lives, are the reason why we feel a certain way; they determine our emotional composition. However, events can never be fully controlled by just us. Things are constantly changing, and there are so many variables in life that can alter an event, and for most people, accordingly alter their mood.

So this raises the question: Why do we let events determine how we feel? Have we not learned that life will be unstable if we approach it in such a way? Are we under the false impression that our emotions cannot be controlled in any other fashion? Too many people have fallen victim to the notion that only circumstances can produce desired emotions. Not enough people have realized that everyone's happiness can be created and controlled when Happiology is mastered!

Consistent happiness can be attained when we focus our energy on the things that we can control. We cannot control all of the circumstances that challenge us every day. We cannot rely on the slim hope that everyone does everything as they are supposed to in order to directly create happiness in our lives. It's literally impossible, and to think otherwise would simply be foolish. For example, a student cannot hope to go to school every day where everybody is affable and the teachers hand out easy A's. Everyone knows that such an assumption would be ridiculous because a student cannot control the behavior of his peers, nor the grading policies and workload of his or her teachers.

So, if we cannot control all of the people and events around us, what must we do to attain happiness? The one and only thing that people have control over that can make them happy just happens to be the most powerful force in the entire world. It's not the billion-dollar technology developed by scientists, nor is it the most powerful medicine being prescribed by doctors. It is without a price tag, is granted to all humans on this planet, and is fully controllable. It is, of course, the human mind.

Everyone is blessed with the most powerful asset they will ever acquire, yet almost everyone takes it for granted. The human mind is the pathway to success and happiness. Unfortunately, most people don't use it to their best capacity. They are under the impression that free and given means decreased value. However, the opposite holds true; all of the things that we were blessed with at birth are the most valuable things we will ever get. Heart, soul, family—the list goes on and on.

The mind can be used for success and happiness because it is the field in which we plant our thoughts. Directly and indirectly, our thoughts hold major influence over the actions and decisions we make. Essentially, they are the ingredients for the human mind. If used properly, they can be utilized to create happiness!

Stop Attending the Pity Party

Have you ever stopped and considered why you do certain things in life? Why do you choose to get up and go to work? Why do you choose to eat food? Why do you choose to spend time with family? Everything you do is because of one ultimate desire that you have (subconsciously or consciously) and it is why you feel good or bad about certain things.

If you haven't realized it already, this goal is to be happy and make your loved ones happy. We all live with this desire. We go to work every day to make money to buy things that we believe will ultimately make us happy. We eat so that our stomach is satisfied and we can enjoy the meal, which makes us happy. We spend time with family, read books, watch television, and go golfing because it makes us happy. The root cause for most of the decisions we make is happiness, for ourselves and those we care about.

Happiness is what all humans naturally desire. So why are so many people still unhappy and miserable, and for what reason do they not attempt to change? For many people, it is because they enjoy feeling bad for themselves. For others, it is simply because they do not know what to do to become happy. However, with a strong commitment and proper application of the Happiology studies in this book, I absolutely assure you that happiness will come to you, and it will last. With this being said, an important factor in your happiness starts right now in the form of a simple decision.

The first and most important step to attaining genuine joyfulness comes right now by simply committing to happiness. One would think this is an obvious given that you are already reading this book, but this is not true. So, first and foremost, **you must decide that you want to be happy under all circumstances.** Reading this book will be a fruitless venture and waste of time if you do not first tell yourself that happiness is what you want and that you are willing to earn it. President Abraham Lincoln once said, "People will often be as happy as they choose to be." It is crucially important to understand that happiness does not just happen; it is a process. *Happiology* will help to guide you and aid you in the development of the skill-set needed to create your happiness.

So many people wallow in self-pity and grief,

complain, or blame others for their unhappiness rather than work toward actually being happy. If they don't get what they want one time, they start complaining and making excuses, saying, "I'm just unlucky," or "I wasn't meant to be happy." They have such horrible attitudes, and they wonder why they are unhappy. The truth is, these people enjoy feeling sorry for themselves. For this reason, many people live their lives unwilling to put forth the effort required to change things and create happiness. Don't let that be you . . . You are the exception!

In other cases, people say, "I'll be happy when . . .," then list events that must first happen before they can be happy. Oftentimes, that which these people seek to be happy never shows up. Other times, it happens, but causes only a short burst of happiness before these people move on to the next event they "need" to be happy. It is a never-ending cycle featuring short periods of happiness and long periods of disappointment and sorrow. True happiness doesn't work this way. Upon reading this book, you will realize that you can be happy at all times, no matter what circumstances you are dealing with.

As a child, like most children, I was always curious about everything. No matter what the situation, I would ask questions and try to figure out the meaning and purpose of things. I wanted answers more than anything. Most people lose this curiosity as they age, but for me, it grew to a bigger and broader concept. This concept was the purpose of life and the importance of happiness.

Toward the end of middle school, I began questioning why I was going through constant ups and downs. I would wonder why my peers, all still in the cliché "best time of their lives," were leading thoroughly unhappy lives. It made no sense to me, and the idea of life and happiness marinated in my mind on a daily basis for years. I realized that happiness is all we actually seek from life, but most people don't know how to attain it! It suddenly occurred to me that so many people actually chose to be unhappy, and I too had fallen victim to this sin of feeling bad for myself at times.

Once I put the pieces together, I realized that a dramatic change was needed, and I began to approach life differently. This led me to making many realizations which will be discussed throughout this book. Basically, it was only after I decided that happiness is what I wanted that I started to actually become happy. It was a transformation from spurts of happiness to lasting happiness. You must also decide to be happy. If you want something, you must first decide that you want it, and then determine just how badly you want it!

Before reading the rest of this book, you should commit yourself to Happiology. The principles and ideologies of this book will be of no use to you unless you first decide that you will make the effort to be happy. Yes, it will be a bit of a struggle to start, but with time, it will become second nature and genuine happiness will be yours with minimum effort.

Happiness is a concept that is greatly misunderstood by most people; it does not come easily. Instead, it comes as a result of work and the development of skills that will help you become happy. You must be willing to change and adjust to some new ways of living as that is the price you pay for eternal joy. Life is not about embarking on the pursuit of happiness; it is about embracing the happiness that comes with the pursuit itself.

Exercise:

1. On the lines below, write that you want happiness and list all that you are willing to do for happiness (change, adjust, etc.). Then, write that you will apply the principles of this book to become happy. Copy the words on an index card, if you choose. Recite the statement every morning upon awakening and every night before sleeping. This will help direct your desire and assure that you know you want to be happy.

_____

_____

_____

_____

_____

_____

The Essential Happiness Ingredient

There's one single aspect of life that can make or break almost anything. It is arguably the single most important factor to becoming happy and successful in life, yet most people do not use it to their greatest advantage. It is not money, cars, clothes, or any tangible object; it is something you can control no matter what set of circumstances life has thrown at you. It is your attitude.

Your way of thinking/your mindset/your approach to life is an indescribably essential factor in your overall happiness and success in whatever it is you want to do. The great motivator Zig Ziglar captured this very concept, once saying, "Your attitude, not your aptitude, will determine your altitude." He asserted that it is not how much you are capable of doing, but instead, how you approach doing something that matters. The importance of your mentality in all walks of life cannot be understated; it is powerful enough, if used properly, to enable you to do anything.

Ziglar hits the nail on the head by making the distinction between capability and attitude/thought process. That is, one can be fully capable of getting a job done in terms of possessing the proper knowledge, skill-set, or physical talent, but if this person lacks a good attitude, the end result will be subpar. On the other hand, if a person does not necessarily possess all talents or skills for a job but does have a great attitude, the products of the work will be superior. This is what causes many employers in the modern world to hire employees with the right attitude, even if they are slightly less qualified than other candidates for the same position.

By definition, attitude is just how a person mentally approaches something. Our thoughts determine how we approach life on an everyday basis and essentially define us. The right attitude is vitally important in a number of ways. Before anything can be physically accomplished, mental action must be taken first. The person must think they can do something prior to actually doing it. Oftentimes, what a person thinks and believes is what actually happens. Our external circumstances are direct results of our thoughts. Consider, for example, the placebo effect. Patients are given a pill, told the medicine is designed to treat the disease they have, and magically get better despite the fact that the pill contains no medicine. Simply by *telling* the patients that they are taking medicine, doctors are able to transform the mindset of the people to the point where they expect to improve from the pill. Oftentimes, people have been physically healed by the placebo effect because of the change in their way of thinking and their belief that they will be cured.

A good attitude is proper utilization and control of the mind, which is a massively powerful weapon for happiness in life. With the right attitude, this weapon can be used for good, but with the wrong attitude, it can cause destruction. Attitude, therefore, is a double-edged sword which we can use as we wish.

The first fundamental change in thinking starts with the base of all of your thoughts. The thoughts we allow our brain to soak up directly reflect what we get out of life, and, in turn, determine our happiness. To be happy, a certain commonality must exist in all of our thoughts so that happiness can be ours, regardless of circumstances. These commonalities are attitudes and thoughts of gratitude and positivity that should be applied to all aspects of life.

From Gratitude Comes Greatness

It is impossible to master the science of creating your happiness without first implementing an attitude of gratitude. That is, being thankful for everything you have is the primary gateway to a stable sense of happiness through all of life's circumstantial ups and downs. Gratitude is the single healthiest human emotion. Once the habit of applying gratefulness to all happenings in life is established, you will be overwhelmed with joy and truly begin to realize just how much you have to be happy for.

Those who can see the beauty of the things they are blessed with every day are much happier than those who do not express their appreciation. The mastery of gratitude is a matter of taking everything that happens to you, especially what most people would take for granted, and being genuinely thankful for it.

Those who can take the worst situation and extract the positivity out of it will earn the happiness they desire. A grateful person can take even the most sorrowful of events and find the meaning for it or the good behind it. An ungrateful person can take the happiest moments and be drowned in sorrow by finding something negative.

Being grateful and positive are similar and often go hand-in-hand. Circumstances are the same for all of us in terms of face value; however, how we choose to perceive them and feel about them is our choice. Decide that you want to be grateful for these circumstances and the creation of happiness becomes simpler and easier!

In math, multiplying two negatives always equals a positive number. This can be applied to how people behave. Some people appear to have been handed two negatives, but they manage to use their attitude of gratitude to find the positive. Other people have something that appears to be positive, but manage to see it as two negatives. Have an attitude that is that of a positive, optimistic, and grateful person, and you will always find that happiness comes to you without a struggle.

You can't always control your circumstances, but you can choose to always be grateful. You can find joy in almost anything if you're willing to look for it. Every event in your life is like a coin, with two sides that you could choose to look at—the good or the bad. It is entirely your choice, and, therefore, there is no one to blame if you feel that life lacks happiness.

I once heard a story of a man who was upset with his wife and was ready for a divorce. Before actually going to that extent, though, he met with a counselor to discuss his marital concerns in private. The unhappy man and the counselor chatted for several hours about the problems and considered potential solutions, but all to no avail. Approaching the end of the session, the counselor posed a question to the miserable spouse: "Do you like anything about your wife?"

The man stopped and thought about the question, coming to the conclusion that there were some things he liked. The counselor encouraged him to name a few. He said he enjoyed her sense of humor and the fact that she was the mother of his children. The counselor pulled out a pad and together they came up with reason after reason as to why the husband loved his wife. The husband, realizing all the wonderful qualities of his spouse he had overlooked due to the recent turbulence, went home with joy that night and began to take concentrated notice at all of the beautiful qualities he loved about his wife.

Long story short, the experience the man had with the counselor changed his attitude, and soon the partners were happy once again. Their minor problems were smoothened out by the strength of a mutual bond of gratitude. While the situation remained the same, the way of approaching the issue had changed. That change solved everything and also helped to save a marriage.

Why are people happier on Fridays or Saturdays as opposed to other days of the week? The happiness comes only from an altered state of mind—a change in attitude due to the day of the week. Preacher Joel Osteen says that every day can be a Friday. We just have to be grateful every day of the week. We can get through any problem if we remember to be grateful for every situation we are put in. You may be thinking that certain situations are impossible to be grateful for. How can I possibly be happy or grateful when I lose my job or a loved one passes away? That's a seemingly valid point, but one that I believe is baseless if we can understand just one basic principle that I'll keep on repeating: Everything in life happens to us for a reason. It is vastly important to understand that something that is happening now is affecting something greater that will be happening later. In this case, the pain of the situations above is worth being grateful for because, if perceived correctly, it makes you stronger and pushes you to grow as a person.

Once you can understand that everything has a positive benefit because everything has a reason behind it, you can find things to be grateful for in everyday life. Think about something you really love. Now think about everything you had to go through to get it. You'll start discovering a series of things that you considered unfortunate at one point in time, but turned out to be good for you and were part of a bigger and better plan. In other words, oftentimes, humans are put into situations they consider unfortunate at the time, but ultimately get something even better. It is important to be grateful for the situations that seem "unfortunate" by acknowledging that everything happens to us for a reason and knowing that every cloud has a silver lining.

I like to think of musicians and artists as examples. Many of them grew up with difficult childhoods and constant struggles. Their backgrounds established foundations for their music and connections with listeners and fans. Everything they went through—all of the pain, all of the problems they fought through and probably couldn't understand—all make sense now. Their difficult past ultimately helped them more than anything in the grand scheme of things.

Pain is something worthy of being grateful for simply because of how it changes you. It makes you stronger and better and prepares you for all that life has to offer. In addition, without pain, there is no great feeling in pleasure. You can't appreciate the sun without the rain, and that's why it is so important to be grateful for everything in life.

When implementing an attitude of gratitude, it is critically important that we do not overlook the small gems of good in our lives that should be appreciated. Too often, the small details of life get taken for granted when they should be appreciated; things get overlooked and are deemed not worthy of our gratitude. Consider all of the minor things you take for granted every day. Whether it is a functioning phone charger or a good television show or something even smaller, there are far too many things that don't get proper recognition. If you start becoming aware of this on an everyday basis, you will find that there are many minor things that are important that you are overlooking. Becoming grateful for these details is critical for the attainment of consistent happiness.

In conclusion, becoming a happy person starts with recognition and appreciation of all that you have been blessed with. Gratitude is the key that unlocks the complete joy that comes with living life, and all it requires is a simple change in our attitude. Promise yourself an attitude of gratitude under all circumstances. Its effects will be seen immediately in your level of happiness.

Exercises:

1. It's extremely important to be grateful mentally, verbally, and physically. That is, we should think about how grateful we are for things, we should tell the world how grateful we are, and we should write about that which we are grateful for. The first two are covered simply by understanding that everything happens for a reason and being thankful. The last one is accomplished by keeping a gratitude journal. Purchase a notebook, label it "Gratitude Journal," and every day list at least five things that you are grateful for that happened on that particular day. Do this every day as a regular part of becoming a happier person. Start your first entry right now:

    1.

    2.

    3.

    4.

    5.

2. Add one item every single day that you can always be grateful for no matter what situation you are in. This list will develop a larger picture of gratefulness for the things that matter most. Start listing ideas below.

-
-
-
-
-
-
-
-
-

3. The last exercise for expressing gratitude has to do with appreciating the people in your life. Whether they are people you like or dislike, find some way to express your gratitude for having them in your life. You can say it to them directly, write them a note, or just tell yourself, but find some way to express your gratitude for everyone in your life. Remember that there is a reason everyone is in your life, and you just need to find a way to be grateful for them. Below, write the names of some people you feel you need to thank and write the way in which you will thank them. Implement the notes you write below as much as you possibly can!

_____

_____

_____

_____

_____

_____

_____

_____

_____

_____

_____

_____

_____

_____

_____

_____

The Power of Positivity

In addition to having an attitude of gratitude, it is also important to live life with a positive mindset. Positivity functions as a virus; even a small dose of positive thoughts will expand exponentially in your mind. Thoughts lead to actions, and actions lead to results. Therefore, happiness, a positive result, comes only as a result of having a positive attitude. Conversely, unhappiness, a negative result, comes only as a result of thinking negatively.

Your attitude toward the world will determine what you get from the world. If you are a positive thinker who seeks the best and expects good things to happen, you will see good, positive things transpiring in your life. On the other hand, if you have a bad attitude and you point out bad luck and make note of how unfortunate your circumstances are, you will continue to see negative happenings. Essentially, how you think determines what you actually get. The mind is immensely powerful, and if used properly, can bring happiness to anyone at any time. Happiness is not a matter of what is happening, but how we approach these happenings. If we can properly utilize our attitude and way of thinking, we will be enabled to take control of our happiness. The reason the aforementioned placebo effect works is because it alters the patients' attitude and causes them to think positively. Despite no medicine being given, the patients believe that their circumstances will change, and this belief alone causes real, physical change. What they think is ultimately what they get. This is a prime example of the power of a mind flooded with positive thoughts.

As many wise men before me have previously analogized, thinking positively is like planting a seed in the ground. Our thoughts are seeds that we plant, and these seeds are what ultimately determine what fruit we get out of life. A positive thought is a seed for a tree that bears sweet fruit, so the more positive thoughts we have, the better.

Naturally, the question one would pose in response to this is, "Why do so many people not fully utilize their ability to control their attitude to their advantage?" It could be that people enjoy basking in sorrow and choose to be unhappy or that they are simply uninformed. Whatever the case, people have a choice between being optimistic or pessimistic in life and, for some odd reason, people tend to choose the latter. It is as if they are actually seeking to not advance forward in life. This is a prime example of people choosing to be unhappy so that they can reserve the right to feel sorry for themselves. It is so important to make the decision to be positive and optimistic, as this is the only way to enjoy the ripest fruits from the tree of life.

One great way to stay positive is to realize that all events that occur in our lives are nothing but events. That is, nothing can be labeled positive or negative until we assign it a connotation. As the famous Shakespeare line goes, "There is nothing either good or bad, but thinking makes it so." It is the way we think that can make us believe that a certain event is good or bad, negative or positive. Human beings take every circumstance in life and deem it "good" or "bad," almost instinctually. This "instinct" needs to become a conscious choice of deciding that every event is positive in order to maintain consistent happiness.

Everything should be interpreted in a positive manner for a higher level of happiness. When you make the decision to start living life with the mindset that everything happens for a reason, thinking negatively will actually become difficult. That is, seemingly bad things will happen, but with a positive mindset, you will be able to recognize problems, learn from them, grow as a person, and ultimately APPRECIATE them. With a negative attitude, problems will be magnified and the situation will ultimately only grow worse.

I like the story of Eric Thomas, a prominent motivational speaker. He is most known for a speech entitled "How Bad Do You Want It?" where he discusses the importance of the burning desire to be successful. He says that his biggest asset was being homeless as it made him stronger and helped him deal with pain. That's a true positive attitude. Most people would take being homeless and expand on it as being a negative thing and use that as an excuse for not tapping into their full potential. Thomas, however, turned the negative into a positive and has risen to become a great modern-day motivational speaker. Every day we have a choice: be positive and learn or be negative and find every excuse as to why we cannot be happy. It's up to us, either way.

It's actually not as difficult as it seems to change our way of thinking. The most important factor is just being willing and understanding that there is always a bigger picture to our lives. Remember, thinking positively is a choice, just as the entire idea of happiness is.

When you wake up in the morning, you've got a choice between spending the day happily, with a positive attitude, or unhappily, with a negative attitude. You must make the clear decision to think positively because many times, by natural instinct, the brain will cling to feeling bad for no reason and create negative thoughts as a result. Negative thoughts, just like positive ones, are viruses. If destroyed early on, they cannot grow or spread and can very easily be corrected.

Norman Vincent Peale, author of *The Power of Positive Thinking*, suggests that we take every negative thought that crosses our mind and kill it, replacing it with a positive thought. This is an excellent strategy, and it is this type of behavior that is instrumental in changing our way of thinking. The effort is critical as this constant positivity will translate to a change in actions and an overall improvement in our quality of life. This is not difficult, but it is not easy either; we just need to make up our minds and decide that we will be positive thinkers.

A major benefit that comes with thinking positively is the ability to avoid paranoia and anxiety. If you've ever been paranoid or anxious in your life, you know that both, especially in conjunction, are absolutely dreadful feelings. In addition, they often come as a result of thinking negatively and over-thinking. Anxiety and paranoia are the result of a wrong attitude. For many people, this becomes a major issue and often has extreme consequences. Many believe that the only escape is some form of medication, but there is a natural remedy—becoming a positive thinker. Educating oneself on the importance of expecting the best out of life is so beneficial that it can and will kill uneasy feelings and allow people to live worry-free. This is crucial to being happy, as constantly fearing all of the bad things that can (but probably won't) happen will lead to a deep sorrow that will fundamentally alter one's ability to enjoy life.

Positive thinking, for some people, can be seen as a daunting task, but it gets easier and easier after you get started. The results are immensely powerful and well worth the effort. Remember, consistent happiness is not about circumstances; it is about the proper attitude. Start becoming positive right now! Cut off all negative voices around you: the people, the TV, the radio. Feed your mind positive things and enjoy the positive results!

Exercises:

1. Create a positive thinking worksheet. On the left-hand side of the page, write an event. In the middle of the page, write the connotation of the event you would normally have—positive, neutral, or negative. Then on the right-hand side, identify all positives from the event that you've noticed that you may have missed the first time. You can do the right-hand side over time, or you can do it immediately, that is up to you. Try to get as many positives in as possible. With time, this will transform your entire way of thinking to the point where finding the positives in life comes naturally and without having to write anything. Here's a little chart to get you started, with an example. You fill out the rest!

EVENT	ORIGINAL CONNOTATION	POSITIVES
Didn't get a job promotion	Negative	Creates opportunity for something better, gives time for improvement, increases focus and drive

2. Write and read something positive before sleeping every night.

Keep a list of positive statements that you want to guide your life. Every night, write down the statements, and then recite them aloud. It is important to write them every single night in order to plant the ideas in your head, and reading them will allow your brain to hear it. Here are some sample statements that you may choose to use. For the blank bullet points, add your own positive statements.

- "I will get a good night's sleep."

- "Tomorrow will be a great day."

- "I can't wait to _____ tomorrow."

-

-

-

-

-

3. Surround yourself with people who are already positive; negativity is extremely contagious. In order to get started with your change in attitude, limit your time with those who think negatively. Find people who are always positive and absorb their way of thinking. In no time, you too will adopt their way of thinking. Then you can open yourself to all groups of people and infect them with positivity as well!

Just Let Go

Have you ever wondered why people say that ignorance is bliss? Many people believe that knowledge is power, so not knowing something (being ignorant) must be a bad thing, right? However, if we define ignorance as selectively choosing to ignore certain things, then ignorance would indeed be bliss. In other words, "ignoring is bliss" because if we carefully decide what to listen to and what to ignore, then we can just let go and be happy. On too many occasions, people allow comments from other individuals to bother them and stop them from doing something. Learning to ignore these people and not be bothered is an art and an incredible skill for all of life's pursuits, especially when it comes to Happiology. Life is full of insignificant people who are always looking to initiate trivial battles. Too often, people engage in these fights when they should really just back off and keep their own peace. It is important to understand that there will always be people who will criticize you, doubt you, condemn you, and say you cannot do something. This is especially true when you are chasing your dreams or pursuing a goal. There are two ways to deal with these people: you could invest countless hours and amounts of energy pointlessly arguing, or you can ignore them and continue on your path. If the person's negative comments are trying to discourage you from following your dreams, then ignore them and keep working hard to prove those people wrong. Forget fruitless bickering and remember that results don't lie. If someone is, in fact, doubting you, don't waste your time arguing. Instead, just keep working for what you know you can accomplish.

Is it really worth your time to argue with that coworker or friend whose comments annoy you? Those who have to comment on your life and those who must judge you are just reflecting their own insecurities. Your desire to become something in life is seen as a threat to many people. As a natural response, those people look to put you down. You must rise above. Never allow an enemy to slow you down, and certainly never get emotionally engaged in an argument that will yield nothing but inner hostility.

Instead of being disturbed by what individuals who dislike you have to say, attain happiness from it. If they say something bad about you, don't get emotionally involved with them. Instead, be grateful that you are not so insecure that you must go around insulting others. This is all about having the right attitude when people try to flood you with negative comments.

If you are about to get upset or angry at the person, just remind yourself that you have chosen to be happy instead. As we've discussed numerous times throughout this book, the decision to be happy comes with change. If you are used to engaging in these trivial fights, it may be hard at first. However, I assure you that if you implement this strategy a few times, and you continue to be positive, that person will stop and you will be the ultimate victor.

Ignoring the small voices that have negative things to say is a good way of cutting negativity from your life altogether. Despite one person's negativity, you must stay positive and remain you. This has two major effects. First of all, you will not be fazed by what someone else has to say. Second, positivity is extremely contagious, so if you overpower a person with your own positive thoughts and sentiments, that person may even change. This would be the ultimate reward of first ignoring, and then implementing the skill of being positive.

The principle of ignoring things is also important in the pursuit of a dream or a series of goals. This is because anytime you are working toward achieving something, people will always try to tell you that you cannot do it, that it is too difficult, or that you are not qualified. There will always be naysayers who try to stop you with their words of discouragement and negativity. Ignore these people and continue pursuing that which you desire. Walter Bagehot, the British journalist and businessman, once said, "The greatest pleasure in life is doing what people say you cannot do." The greatest pleasure is not feeding into your critics' words and helping them grow, but rather ignoring them and then pursuing your dreams so that your actions can speak for you! Learn to ignore the pointless battles that people try to lure you into. This will make you happier and aid you in staying at peace!

Some people in this world will always be negative, especially to those who are happy or successful. They'll always argue with you and try to bring the worst out of you. You could do anything for them, but they will always find a way to point out the bad. These are the exact people who must be ignored and, if possible, cut out from your life altogether. Zig Ziglar once said, "The only taste of success some people will get is by taking a bite out of you." You should think of that bite as a compliment!

Imagine if Albert Einstein gave up his pursuit of excellence just because people told him he would be nothing. After all, it wasn't until age 4 that Einstein could speak. Many people were certain he had some sort of disability. Teachers said he would never be anything in life. If Einstein, even at such a young age, had listened to those who said he would be nothing, imagine how far back the field of science in general would be! No one believed Einstein would be anything, especially when he was young, but he didn't care. He just ignored them, carried on, and ended up changing the world with his discoveries.

One would think it's almost a given that we should not be distracted by insignificant voices, but most of us are affected by them to some extent. You must develop a way to ignore these negative comments and prove naysayers wrong with a serving of success. As the saying goes, "Kill them with success and bury them with a smile."

Exercises:

1. Make a note below declaring that you will not allow smaller voices to pester or distract you. Start it with "I declare that . . ." and end it with ". . . in my pursuit of (a goal)." Do this with multiple goals if you choose to. An example would be, "I declare that I will ignore all belittling voices that try to discourage me in my pursuit of becoming a lawyer."

_____
_____
_____
_____
_____
_____
_____

2. Simply ignore and remain positive when you are flooded with negativity by someone or some group of people. I'm sure that right now, in your head, you know someone who often causes you trouble with their negativity. List the names of such people below and make it a point to not allow their behavior get to you.

The Present is a Present

One of the biggest causes of unhappiness among people nowadays is incredibly simple. Most people even overlook it when they consider why they are unhappy about a situation. The problem is that people do not live in the present moment. Their physical actions and mental processes are almost never in sync. People have grown so accustomed to physically being in one place and mentally being in another that they've essentially lost the ability to truly live happily. Have you ever stopped and noticed just how often your mind is dwelling on lingering memories of the past or creating images of the future? Unfortunately, humans spend most of their time focusing on something that has happened or has yet to happen. This way of thinking causes unhappiness, but can be transformed into one of the best tools for consistent happiness. Jim Rohn's advice was priceless: "When at work, work. When at play, play."

As established earlier, our thoughts are the core of who we are and what we do, and those very thoughts are what ultimately determine our happiness. A mind infatuated with the unchangeable past or possibly unfortunate future will never be liberated from the chains of negative thoughts that enslave the mind and restrict happiness.

Thinking about the past or future to reflect, learn, and/or plan is perfectly fine and is actually needed. It is actually a positive thing, but we cannot let our minds think too much about either one. Remember, the most precious gift there is, is free and priceless—the present moment. Constant over-thinking about the past or the future will assuredly cause us to become unhappy and lose our grip on living for right now. Ralph Waldo Emerson once said, "With the past I have nothing to do; nor with the future. I live for now." He captures the essence of what living in the present is with that assertion. We must make a concentrated effort to live for now and program our minds to soak up the present for consistent happiness.

Oftentimes, it is human nature to reflect on the past and be overwhelmed with worry, regret, or sorrow. We must realize that the past is over and what has happened is done with. Instead of worrying about what could have been or what should have happened, be positive. Rather than regret the events of the past, learn from them and adjust to a new way of living. Forget about what happened, but never forget what you learned. Then, utilize what you learned to further embrace the present moment.

Always remember that every circumstance life has thrown at you has happened for a reason. Instead of saying, "I'm just unlucky, things never work out for me," start learning and recognizing that everything is happening for a reason. Quit feeling sorry for yourself, as most people love to do, and work to become a happy person. Don't let the past control your mind. As the saying goes, "The past is a good place to visit, but I wouldn't want to live there." Do not allow what has happened to control who you are and how you behave in the present time.

Everything works itself out with time so don't stress yourself out over the past since it happened for a reason. In fact, if you learn to stay positive with faith, you will realize the reason for why something has happened. Maybe the person you liked so much wasn't who you thought they were or that job opportunity wasn't actually the best thing for you. Oftentimes, we get something better than what we were expecting, and then we become grateful that the thing we were initially wishing for didn't happen. If you look back at how certain things have happened in the past, you will realize that there was a distinct reason for them happening the way they did. You will find that the past was actually a positive thing when a mindset of appreciation and learning is instilled within you. What has happened has happened, and with time and a proper attitude, you will be able to learn from the past to maximize your ability to live in the present.

Another reason people struggle to live in the present is because they get caught up in imagining the future. Many people worry about what might happen, when the reality of the matter is that there is absolutely no way of telling what the future holds. Things can change circumstantially in an instant, and you cannot allow yourself to follow that wave of change with your emotions. If you constantly look to the future and keep on clinging to a fantasy of what life will be like, you will never learn to appreciate what life actually is. A mind that lives in the future all the time won't be able to fully enjoy life in the present moment.

It is great to have goals and a plan of action for the future, but it is pointless to spend the present moment worrying and stressing out over a future that you do not know. Set goals, work hard to achieve them, and then leave the rest; the fruits of your labor will come. Quit worrying and recognize that your future is safe if you just work hard and keep faith that things will work themselves out. Recognize it, appreciate it, and stay worry-free. Those who have a true faith in the future don't worry about it; they are naturally happy and naturally hopeful.

Stay hopeful for the future while living in the present and learning from the past. With this simple philosophy engrained in your mind, you will forever be freed from the burdens of constantly thinking about what has occurred and/or what will happen.

If you take this information seriously, you will be freed from living in the past or overly concerned about the future. However, to say that you are not thinking about the past or future is not to say that you are living in the present. To achieve the syncing of what you are doing physically and what you are thinking mentally is a larger challenge. It does not come easily, but can happen with practice and concentrated effort. This all goes back to making the decision to be happy. It is worth the effort, however, because one who is able to master the art of living in the present will always be happy.

Consider the noteworthy characteristics of those who live in the present. You will find that these people tend to be at ease most of the time and are extremely aware of where they are and what they are doing.

They tend to concentrate better and have a peaceful aura about them as a result of the gratefulness they possess from simply living and embracing life. Notice, these are the rare qualities that everyone seeks to have, and they all come as a result of learning to live in the present. Do you possess this quality? If not, would you like to? Of course you would! That's why it is worth making the effort!

Mastering this art is a bit of a process in the beginning, but with time it becomes easier. It is crucially important to clear out irrelevant thoughts about all other things and concentrate your focus on what you are doing right now. With every step you take, be consciously aware and fully mindful of it. Instead of mindlessly walking with no re-alization of what you are doing, recognize and feel your foot hitting the earth. See and feel the nature around you and be fully aware of the present moment!

You must understand that every moment you live on this planet is unique; it will never happen again. Be grateful for every single moment as best you possibly can. Naturally, you will be grateful and start to recognize all that you have been blessed with. Start this process very slowly if you must, but always try to be consciously aware and mindful of what you are doing. Be aware and be happy about the opportunity to do it.

You will most likely have to begin this with basic actions such as simply walking and breathing. Clear your mind with a deep breath and keep things simple to live for right now. In the beginning, it is important to con-stantly remind yourself that you are living in the present. This is the only way it will become a regular habit. If you do this enough with the right commitment to being hap-py, you will most certainly be happier more often and be able to establish a consistent joyfulness in your life.

Exercises:

1. Oftentimes, the biggest mistake made when trying to live in the present is forgetting to actually do it, especially in the beginning. The mind is an amazingly powerful tool, so, of course, transforming its fundamental nature will take practice. So, in your own words, write a few sentences below about how you will eliminate the past and future from your mind and concentrate on living in the present. Read the sentences three times a day till they become second nature.

_____

_____

_____

_____

_____

_____

_____

2. Embrace everything you can in life. Be patient and be consciously aware of everything that you are doing. This is immensely important in becoming consistently happy. Doing this will also help you forget the past and the future and stay focused on the present. Here are some situations and examples of how you should embrace them. I have filled two out; you fill out the rest.

Situation	Living in the Present
Writing an essay on a computer	~ Feel every key as you press it ~ Concentrate on every word you spell out
Drinking tea	~ Taste every sip of the drink (drink slowly) ~ Feel the temperature of the drink and be appreciative of the quality of it
Walking	
Sitting	
(Your Choice)	

The Simpler, the Better

With society advancing at such a rapid pace, it is easy to get caught up in all of the new and complex things that are being introduced to us. Many of us are led to believe that the more complex something is, the better it is. However, complexity often means stress that takes away from our happiness in life. Simplicity is important in a variety of ways. From the amount of thought put into one subject area to the vocabulary we use to the way we dress ourselves, the simpler things are, the easier it is to be happy.

Society tends to promote the idea that the greater the complexity, the greater the product. People make it seem as if nothing great can be had without an immense amount of effort and stress first being put into it. Yet, the opposite is true; just as Confucius once said, "Life is really simple, but we insist on making it complicated." The common person believes that there must be something difficult or complicated, that nothing can really be accomplished in a simple manner, but to truly be happy, it makes a lot more sense to just keep things simple.

Consider the books people enjoy reading. The underlying difference in our reading preferences can often be found in the complexity of the books. An example of this would be why so many students enjoy reading *The Great Gatsby* as opposed to *The Adventures of Huckleberry Finn*. The former is much easier to understand because of its simple nature, while the latter is far more complicated. This same principle can be applied to people as well—those who are simpler overall tend to be happier and lead easier lives.

Leading a simpler life starts with the reduction of that which is unnecessary. There are very few things that we actually need in life. Many things can be cut out mentally and physically, and the result will be the attainment of greater happiness. As you read this, think of the various ways you can make your own life simpler!

The first place this reduction takes place is in your mind. As noted throughout the book, the human mind is easily the most powerful tool on the planet, so it must be used properly. Sticking to this ideology, it is important to not overload the mind with things that it does not need to be thinking about. The mind is the workplace for the body, and it should not be cluttered with unnecessary ideas. Retaining knowledge and learning facts are absolutely excellent, but it is critically important to not over-think and keep situations in your head simple.

I cannot stress the immense importance of not over-thinking something. Over-thinking is the core root of nearly all unhappiness. People think so much about something that they lose their grip on the present moment and create negative scenarios that will never actually occur. Quit painting negative pictures of the future in your head and stop worrying about what might happen. Concentrate on the positive and stay focused on what is actually happening.

People use their minds for the worst when they think about things too much. This is why it is so important to keep things in your head simple and to take everything for what it is. Most of the time, the negative visions that we have for the future never actually happen. So why worry and over-think?

Scientists have done various studies on the idea of thinking too much and have come to some important conclusions. For example, 90 percent of the time, over-thinking leads to negative thoughts and can cause disruption to the point of insomnia. In addition, **86 percent of all unhappiness and stress stems from over-thinking.** As discussed earlier, positive thinking is so vital to being happy, and over-thinking often kills that positivity.

To be happy, the first major step is to correct the way

the brain functions. This can only happen by eliminating unneeded and negative thoughts and allowing the brain to function in a simpler manner. There is truly nothing good that will come from exaggerating a situation and creating various scenarios that will never happen. Instead, keep things simple while maintaining faith that things will work themselves out.

The best way to not over-think is just to force yourself to live for the moment and not allow your thinking to get out of hand. As soon as you realize you are exaggerating a situation and are becoming unhappy as a result, repeat some exercises from the chapter on living in the present and keep reminding yourself that you must control your thoughts. Eventually, over-thinking won't even be an issue.

In addition to simplicity in the mind, we should conduct our lives simply physically as well. We must behave simply in terms of how we approach life with the way we do things. You don't have to work hard to get something done if you just work smart and find the simplest way to answer the most complex of questions. If we keep things simple and go about our lives in an uncomplicated manner, things will be much easier. Bill Gates once said that he hires the laziest people to do the most difficult of jobs, since that's how it will get done in an easy and simple manner. The bottom line is: the simpler, the more effective. No, I am not advocating laziness, just simplicity. Simplicity is also fundamental in effective communication. Instead of using a bunch of decorated words for the sake of coming across as some scholar, we must speak in an understandable manner so that both your and the listeners' lives become easier. Certain situations will require us to speak in an extremely formal manner, but whenever possible, we must try to speak simply. Follow this rule with your next business proposal or at a meeting. Stay strong with your message, but non-complex with your choice of words. Make your points compelling but understandable, and watch how much better the presentation becomes! This way of living creates little advantages like this all the time and therefore enhances overall happiness.

Another major benefit of living life simply is the fact that there becomes a lot less to worry about altogether. For example, if you don't have many clothes to choose from (a simple wardrobe) and you avoid buying many unnecessary products (a simple lifestyle), there are less options and therefore, less worry. Have you ever wondered why the rich and famous in society are often unhappy despite having so much? It's because they have more than enough to maintain a luxurious lifestyle and so they go over the top, leading complicated lives. They lack the ability to keep things simple, and the result is that they prove the saying right: money does *not* buy happiness. You, however, by reading this chapter and the rest of *Happiology: The Science of Creating Your Happiness*, have chosen to enrich and energize your life with happiness. Simplicity, of course, is one of the keys most people overlook, but luckily for you, you know better! Keep life simple in all ways, and you will immediately see the benefits!

Exercises:

1. Stop yourself from over-thinking by constantly being in control of your thoughts. Drill yourself on the principles of living in the present and do not dwell too much on one topic. When you find yourself over-thinking, force yourself to perform an exercise from the past chapter and avoid thinking about whatever you were previously dwelling on.

2. Cut out things you think you do not need in your life that are interfering with your ability to live life simply. Start by taking your collection of clothes and donating what you think you will not wear often and is unnecessary. Next, go around your room or home and dispose of things that are not needed. Live life simply by making the most of only that which you need. Luxury is good, but don't let the glamour of too much interfere with your internal peace and happiness. Brainstorm some ways you can make your life simpler and write them down below. Then make sure you execute them!

   -
   -
   -
   -
   -
   -
   -
   -

Be GOAL-den

One of the most underrated factors in happiness is knowing what you want and realizing what you are working toward. A simple, yet essential Happiology key is deciding what you want and committing to attaining that desire. You'd be surprised at how many people live their lives without a purpose and without knowledge of what they desire from their actions. On the surface, it seems that this is too fundamental a step to living to ignore, but it is true that too many people live their lives without any direction. These people lack a tremendously important aspect of being happy as well as successful: goals.

Goals are clear desires that we seek to attain, and as a result, they are what we work toward every day in an effort to achieve. Having goals is very important as it gives us direction in terms of how to live, justifies why we do things, and helps us remember what truly matters in life. A goal is something specific that we have in mind for attaining and is something we must entirely commit to. Goals are what allow us to have some flow to living.Normally, goals are only associated with the career aspect of a person's life. In order to be happy, we must have goals that are diverse and balanced between work, school, social life, family, etc. This is because goals give us direction.

There's no point in doing anything without knowing what the ultimate end desire is. If you know what you ultimately want, then you will be able to understand what steps must be taken. As a result, more meaning will be added to everything you do because there is a vision of something greater that the future holds. All of your actions ultimately reflect this. When you decide what your goals are, your actions in life then have real purpose.

I cannot stress how essential it is to simply know what you want. If you don't know what you are pursuing, you will not see any results or bear any fruit from life. If a student works very hard every day in school to get A's in every honors and AP class, but does not know *why* he or she is working so hard, that student is essentially living without perspective. The student is getting good grades because he/she knows it is important to be "smart," but if they don't know what they ultimately desire as a result of those good grades (a particular college, a specific job, self-pride, etc.), then there is nothing significant behind working hard. In this case, the student will not be happy with the good grades he or she is getting until the student first identifies *why* they are getting the grades and how the grades contribute to a clear and defined goal. Happiness from achievement is produced directly as a result of that achievement contributing to or achieving a goal.

When setting your goals, understand that there is no limit to what you can become or what you can achieve if you are willing to work. Stretch your imagination for whatever it is you want, for you are capable of achieving anything. Don't let anyone say you cannot; if you can dream it and believe in it, then you can do it. Dreaming big and working for your dreams allows you to constantly have something worth striving for. Don't be afraid to be unrealistic, either. Nothing is impossible, and despite what people like to say, what you can believe, you can achieve. The first step on this road, however, is knowing where the destination is and what stops will be on the way. Again, not only should you be happy upon accomplishing a goal, but you should also apply the other Happiology studies to make the pursuit joyful as well. Dreaming big is also important because, without a certain vision for what you want, life can become a long, dry path without a purpose. Many people who go through a midlife crisis in their 40s ascribe the root of the problem to a feeling of disappointment and feeling that they are without a purpose. They stopped setting goals and constantly pouring their heart into working for something, and the result was immense sorrow. Compare those people to little children who are unadulterated by the naysayers of the world and hold lofty ambitions and desires, vowing to become presidents, scientists, and businessmen. They are so happy with that which they seek to achieve because they have goals (even though they may not know it) and they believe they can accomplish them. They may not have a defined plan to make their dreams a reality just yet, but they know what they want and they look forward to having it. Ask yourself, which situation would you rather be in? One with a defined goal that gets you where you want or one that gets you someplace someday but is not of your liking? Goals hold immense power: a life filled with the constant achievement of various goals is filled with happiness.

Instead of pursuing people or money, pursue goals that will help you get better through personal accomplishment. The great Albert Einstein once said, "If you want to live a happy life, tie it to a goal, not to people or things." No material object or person can truly make you happy for your entire life. They may give you small bursts of happiness, but the way to maintain happiness for an extended period of time is by constantly having new and interesting goals that keep life fresh and worth living. Set some destinations on where you want to see yourself, and the journey of life will instantly become something of greater value to you. At the end of the day, we are all traveling on the road of life, and we must have a map of where we are going. Without that road map, it is very easy to get lost and become stressed, unhappy, or even depressed.

Beyond knowing what you want, there are some other steps that must be taken in this process. First of all, these goals must be written down. It is absolutely critical that the mind is always absorbed in your goals, as it then becomes much easier to constantly be working toward achieving them. Writing the dreams and visions down with all of the specifics allows you to clearly express what you want from life. It assures that you have a good understanding of what you actually want and lets you adjust your sail when the ship seems to be straying off course.

With time, after engaging in some of the exercises that I will mention later in the chapter, your vision will become clear and your path to success will be paved. When you have nothing else, you will have these goals that you can always work toward, and no one can ever take that away from you. When life seems like it's at its hardest, your ambition and your desire to become something and attain something from life will keep you going. That is the power of having written goals!

I've heard many stories of people who went through a deep depression at some point in their lives, but kept going because they had dreams, hopes, and visions that one day things will get better and what they desire will be theirs. We all must have goals so strong and powerful that they make life meaningful. Determine what you want, develop a plan, and don't ever let anyone, including yourself, take that dream away from you.

The former outstanding baseball player Yogi Berra explained, "If you don't know where you're going, you'll end up someplace else." Simply put, goals give you the directions to your desired destination. If you don't know what you want from life, how will you ever be happy? If you keep leading your life not knowing where you're going, you'll never even know when you've arrived. You wouldn't get into your car without knowing exactly where you want to go, would you? Why, then, would you want to live your life without a plan for the destination which you desire? Luckily, you are on the right track because you decided you wanted happiness and took action by picking up the right book to learn how to create it!

Goals also, quite obviously, should range in terms of the time period they are projected to be completed in. Short-term, midterm, and long-term goals help to establish a sense of where you are going at all times. Oftentimes, the completion of a long-term goal is simply the coming together of various smaller goals which have been accomplished. A variety of ranges in time and the stretching of goals across all aspects of life will give meaning to literally everything you do and keep you focused on what you want.

Through everything, though, always remember that the decisions you make are ultimately because you want to be happy. Don't wait to be happy when you reach your goals, be happy while you are reaching your goals! Never forget that your ultimate desire in life is to be happy in an ethical and moral way. So often we lose sight of this simple concept and in doing so, become unhappy. Quit doing things for no reason, and start having some purpose while remembering that whatever it is you want does indeed aid in your overall happiness. The ultimate goal is for you to be consistently happy and make the most out of your life. Always remember: Life is like a game of soccer; you cannot win without goals.

Exercises:

1. Think about what you want from life in all respects: education, work, social life, etc., and consider the time for each of these goals as well. Then for each separate goal, write down what the goal is, when you plan on achieving it, what you will sacrifice to achieve it, and what you will gain as a result of achieving it. Then, list some things that will help you achieve the goal. Essentially, make a clear and specific plan for action that you will commit to taking. Read this statement aloud at least twice a day, and be sure to do follow this process for all of your goals. This is essentially an exercise Napoleon Hill talks about in one of my favorite books, *Think and Grow Rich*. Jot down your first few goal statements below, and never forget to make happiness a part of each.

_____

_____

_____

_____

_____

_____

_____

_____

_____

_____

_____

_____

2. In addition to having goals, it is important to have vision and the belief that the BIG things you desire will come true. Pick out your biggest goal, the one you center most of your attention on, and start putting yourself in a situation where it's a given that what you want will happen. For example, if you want to be a top salesman in an industry, start creating awards that say you have already won, along with the year you expect to win. Expect greatness; expect your goals to come to fruition. It may sound corny, but it goes a long way in making sure you stay focused and achieve your goals. Write down some ideas in the lines below, and actually implement them! Make them BIG and BOLD, and work toward making your dreams a reality!

_____

_____

_____

_____

_____

_____

_____

_____

_____

_____

_____

_____

_____

Take Risks, Take Advantage

Throughout this book, we've discussed how important it is to create our happiness by mentally adjusting to things and changing our way of thinking. Although these are the main pathways to joy, we must also take some additional action so that we can fully utilize this new way of thinking. Taking risks and seizing life's opportunities are two of these very important actions. The former often helps to create the latter, and both work together to help create happiness.

The great Ellen DeGeneres once said, "When you take risks, you learn that there will be times when you succeed and there will be times when you fail, and both are equally important." She shed light on the idea that when we do the things that we are uncomfortable with, the results will vary in terms of success. The key, however, is to take the chance that anything can happen and be happy with the ultimate result. If the risk turns out to be something clearly positive, be grateful that you made the decision to do something that first scared you. If the result is seemingly negative, then don't bask in your sorrow; instead, be grateful for the failure and learn for the future. As long as you follow these guidelines, you will be able to grow as a person and enjoy a heightened sense of happiness as well.

This notion falls in line with the idea of seizing opportunities that life has for us. Taking risks is just taking advantage of something we have been offered, but have been afraid to pursue. Most of the time, opportunities are present, but we either fail to recognize them or fear the risk that comes with accepting them.

I encourage you to start taking risks in the form of seizing the opportunities that life has given you. The problem with most people is that they feel opportunities must be handed to them for them to even consider acting on them. The fact remains that with just a little effort, these people could easily find that there is a world of opportunity to explore. You cannot hope for opportunity to just come to you; you must actively search for opportunities. Explore for the chance, find the opportunity, and take the risk; ultimately, growth and happiness will occur.

The thing that stops most people from going out and exploring the world for risks to take and opportunities to seize is the fear that resides in their minds. Fear is merely a state of mind; once we can control fear, we can do anything we want in life. People often make the mistake of over-thinking, which, as talked about earlier, only leads to negative thoughts. These negative thoughts then stop them from taking a risk. Sadly, these people consider everything that could go wrong if they take a risk and often exaggerate the consequences if they take action. Most people need to realize the truth about taking risks and overcome the myth. It is not something to be scared of; it is something to embrace. That which we fear is that what we must conquer.

Risks create growth. Society would never change if no one ever did anything different, if nobody was willing to go out and take a risk. On a personal level, taking risks and seizing opportunities should not be something like running around in traffic—mindlessly scurrying the streets is a risk indeed, but it is not a smart and calculated risk. For each person in society, what scares them will vary, and we must face those things that we think will actually help us grow as people. For example, if you are a businessman and you fear both public speaking and skydiving, then the risk you would take first is engaging in some type of activity that forces you to speak publicly, like participating in Toastmasters. Both risks will cause you to grow as a person, but public speaking will allow you to take a risk while also doing something that is logical for growth in your profession. For now, it would make more sense to take the calculated risk that will be more helpful to you in the immediate future.

People usually think of something bold and crazy when they think of risk taking, but a risk is simply doing something different that you would normally shy away from. Take advantage of opportunities by engaging in what you find challenging, interesting, and scary. This will help you become more open emotionally and become more diverse in that which you have done. As a result of experimenting, exploring, and engaging, you will be consistently happier as well. Just think about it— if you are able to conquer that which you once feared or shied away from, how could you not be happier?

The key to taking risks is committing to it. You must be willing to do things differently for the chance to get something different. People are often so desperate for something to just come to them that they don't realize they must first do something. Happiness is a choice, and so is everything we decide to do in life. If you make the conscious choice to do different and challenging things for the purpose of helping yourself grow, you will get what you want. Simply committing and telling yourself that you will get whatever it is you desire is a good start to taking risks.

Effective risk-taking leads to more opportunities. One of the best ways to create opportunities is to try things you normally wouldn't. The risks you take will introduce you to new experiences. One good decision will lead to many more chances for things that are even better, and this will function as a chain reaction. If you take advantage of the opportunities, you will be able to grow as a person. Either you will enjoy success or you will face failure, but both will ultimately be good for you if you have the right attitude. No matter how it is looked at, taking risks and seizing the opportunities that follow are positive action steps that must be taken for personal growth and happiness.

Much of life is just determining what you want and deciding that you will get it. In this case, since you are reading this chapter, you have decided that happiness is what you want. In order to fulfill this desire, taking risks and seizing opportunities is an absolute must. You will be a conqueror of your fears rather than a scared victim, and you will attain what you desire at the same time.

Exercises:

1. Create a list of things that you often shied away from or have been afraid of. Identify the ones that you think will help you in your growth if you were to conquer them. Then, take this new list and do those things that scare you (public speaking, heights, etc.). At your own pace, get the whole list done.

   -
   -
   -
   -
   -
   -
   -
   -
   -

2. Find your opportunities. After you know what you want in a particular area of your life (social, personal, financial, etc.), explore the world for opportunities that will help you get what you want and help you grow as a person at the same time. Write down what you want, and then list possible ideas for ways you can find opportunities for them. For example, if you want to be a better tennis player, find tennis camps, a trainer, and present yourself in situations that will open you up to even more opportunities by competing in tournaments, etc. Fill out the table below with things you want and ways you will create and seize opportunities for yourself.

What You Desire	Opportunities You Will Create	How These Opportunities Will Help You

Learn to Learn
(Every Single Day)

Growing up as children and young adults, the center of most of our lives is school and the concept of learning. Day in and day out, school must be attended in order to absorb information and become educated individuals. After formal education is over, however, most people give up the act of learning altogether. Whether school is in session or not, we must constantly be learning new things on a daily basis. Most people do not realize that learning is absolutely essential for anyone who wants to keep their mind fresh and grow as a happy person. Nowadays, it is even more important because the world is advancing quickly, forcing us to constantly upgrade our knowledge.

The great businessman Henry Ford stated, "Anyone who stops learning is old, whether at twenty or eighty."

Anyone who keeps learning stays young from a mental standpoint. Constant learning leads to a sharper mind, the broadening of horizons, the creation of new thoughts, and improved self-image and self-confidence. Very much underrated, but critical for overall happiness and success, learning is the key to unlocking hundreds of thousands of doors of opportunity.

Knowledge will set you free as you will be exposed to captivating information that will keep your mind positively engaged and contribute to your overall growth. It consists of two parts—factual learning of history and present time, and behavioral learning for self-improvement. The former helps develop formal education, and the latter helps you break out of your shell to become a greater, happier individual.

With this being said, all learning begins with curiosity and the desire to learn. The path to the attainment of knowledge begins by simply asking questions and wanting answers. It only requires a few minutes a day, and, in turn, the benefits we reap are worthwhile.

If I asked you to list the basic things you do every day, you'd probably say go to school/work, watch some TV, read, cook, use the computer, talk to friends/family, work out, play sports, and other things of this nature. Although you may not realize it, the underlying similarity among these everyday activities is your ability to learn from them. Everything you do, every person you meet, you can and should learn from! As mentioned previously, you should gain two types of information from all of these activities: (1) factual information regarding a particular subject and (2) behavioral knowledge that will help you improve yourself. Here's an example:

Work/Gathering—These events almost always involves reciprocal activity with peers. An environment such as an office tends to be heavy in talking and communicating with others. This is an excellent opportunity to gain knowledge! When you talk to someone, you can learn plenty. First of all, direct knowledge can be gained. The person could forthrightly state a fact like, "The sky is blue." This is direct information that was transferred quickly and easily. Also, in this environment, improving yourself could (and should) come from simply listening to the vocabulary and sentence structure of a statement. One could learn about how something was said or phrased and use this to improve themselves. This type of learning may seem outlandish and unusual, but it requires minimal effort and aids a person a great deal in bettering themselves. The better you become, the more satisfied and happy you will be with yourself.

In almost any situation, learning can be done, such as in the scenario above. As another example, I enjoy speaking to my attorney cousin Vikki, my cousin and mentor. I examine how he carries himself in a conversation when speaking to him, and as a result, I learn a lot. Some is direct, but more of it is from the vocabulary and phrases he uses. In turn, I apply them to my everyday life. It works very well, and it helps me grow and develop. The constant growth helps me maintain a level of happiness, just as it would with anyone who applied the skill. All it really requires is the willingness to learn.

Along with the way someone speaks, everyone can learn from how someone else carries themselves. There's a lot that can be learned if we just analyze things about the people in our lives that we admire. Whether it be the way someone smells or how confident they are, there is something special in everyone. Pick it out and learn from it! Be yourself, but be ready to improve yourself at the same time.

I do this with people all the time. If I like something about them, I adopt that which they do differently in order to improve myself, and I notice that I become happier with myself. You can even apply this skill to characters on TV shows. If there is something about the way they behave that seems superior to what you're doing, learn by watching and adopt it. It is so important to leverage the ability to learn in any situation in order to ultimately become happier.

In addition to learning from what people do well, we can learn from other people's current or past mistakes. The classic Confucius example goes, "If I am walking with two other men, each of them will serve as my teacher. I will pick out the good points of the one and imitate them and the bad points of the other and correct them in myself." Just as we learn from those who are doing it correctly, we must also learn from those who are making mistakes so that we can improve ourselves. Life demands constant development, thus making the ability to learn in all situations and from all people golden in importance. The fact is, the most we will ever learn comes from the mistakes, not successes, of both others and ourselves.Most people know how to learn from their own mistakes, but few think to learn from the mistakes of others. If you are watching a basketball game or chess match, consider the results from both points of view. After examining how the winning team won, find out how the losing team lost and make sure you do not commit those same mistakes. This dual style of learning is far more effective as it helps you improve from both ends of the spectrum (failure and success). If you are a salesperson and want to increase your productivity, converse with a seasoned veteran. In addition to discussing direct ways to success, address and analyze mistakes they made in the past. Now, through one conversation, you have both tips for becoming successful and ways to avoid making certain mistakes. Of course, this way of learning is applicable to all professions.

It is essential to understand that everyone on this planet is an asset to us. Everyone knows something we don't, and every person makes mistakes that are worth learning from. Just as we would learn from the good things someone does, we must analyze the bad things as well for ultimate growth. Experience is the father of wisdom, so when we invest our time to gain knowledge from others, we can become wiser, smarter, and better equipped for an overall happier life.

Society is also so far technologically advanced that we possess many ways of quick and easy learning. We should take full advantage of the fact that we are blessed with phones, computers, tablets, and other devices that can be accessed with just a click. We can turn on the television and find various programs where we can learn about things that we have never even heard of before. Bookstores and libraries across the globe offer consumers the opportunity to come in and read without even purchasing. People would do so much for the opportunities modern-day society has, so don't take it for granted! The great President Abraham Lincoln used to dig through the trash as a clerk to find spare pages of books just to learn about law and develop his knowledge. Today, we can find that information with minimal effort. We must embrace this convenience and take advantage of our opportunity to learn with such ease.

It's crystal clear that learning can be done every day in a variety of fashions—from other people to books to computers to mistakes; there are so many ways to grow as a person every day. With this growth will come various benefits, the most prominent being a heightened sense of happiness. I'll leave you with a Helen Keller quote that captures the concept very well:

"Knowledge is power. Rather, knowledge is happiness, because to have knowledge—broad, deep knowledge—is to know true ends from false, and lofty things from low. To know the thoughts and deeds that have marked man's progress is to feel the great heartthrobs of humanity through the centuries; and if one does not feel in these pulsations a heavenward striving, one must indeed be deaf to the harmonies of life."

Exercises:

1. Every day, make it a priority to learn something from as many people as you come in contact with. Make a chart like the one below and fill in the information. Continue creating charts like this until you naturally learn from people (direct knowledge or how they behave) without having to write it down. Start today using this chart.

Person learned from (Name/ description)	What was learned (Factual/Way of behavior)	How it was learned (Conversation/ observation, etc.)

2. Utilize your ability to learn with ease by keeping a learning journal. This journal will serve as a quick tool for you to learn from the many sources you have available to you. In it, jot down a few facts about anything you have learned, whether it be about history, current events—anything. Add to this notebook daily facts that are meaningful to you and growth by knowledge will occur immediately. You will notice a greater amount of happiness with this increase in knowledge as well. Use the space below to start finding and writing down some facts.

_____

_____

_____

_____

_____

_____

_____

_____

_____

_____

_____

_____

_____

_____

_____

_____

_____

_____

Be-YOU-tiful

Ralph Waldo Emerson once asserted, "To be yourself in a world that is constantly trying to make you something else is the greatest accomplishment." In today's society, people tend to stop being themselves because they are so heavily influenced to be like the people around them. To retain the quality of being yourself is a great accomplishment that is essential for mastering Happiology. Every individual in the world is naturally unique. Still, most people do not capitalize on their chance to be something other than the majority of the population. It is truly baffling how people make an effort to be someone or something they're not. Since so many people want to be the stereotypical definition of "normal" or "regular," being yourself highlights your individuality even more. Being yourself helps you become happier because you are not forcing anything and just embracing your natural identity.

As you learn to stay yourself in spite of a society that is constantly trying to change you, you will realize how much happier you are as a person. You won't be worried about what other people think and living life won't become such an effort, thus making everything simpler. Being yourself is therefore a blessing that should not be easily given up.

Our minds are constantly being polluted by this notion that if we're not like everyone else then we won't be accepted by society. This is humorously ironic because of the lack of truth in the statement. The actual fact is that the leaders and great people of civilization were the ones who weren't afraid to be themselves. These people did not care how other people behave, and that's what allowed them to excel in life. In order to be happy, you too must adopt this mentality.

The only way to live a truly pure life is by being you, because otherwise, you're just misleading yourself. It is hard to believe a person that is consistently dishonest, so imagine the deleterious effects of self-inflicted, intentional lying to oneself. Not being yourself causes internal disruptions, including emotional instability, low self-esteem, and not believing in yourself. It will gnaw at you and disturb every facet of your life. You won't be a good decision maker, and you won't be good at socializing. Why? Because you're going to be relying on other people. We are creatures of habit; if you constantly rely on others for the decisions you must make, like the way you talk, eat, walk, and even think, then you're always going to be dependent on people, even for your happiness! This makes it critically important to cleanse the mind of these kinds of thoughts.

Not being yourself holds you back tremendously in many aspects of life. If you have to do what everyone else is doing, you're putting a cap on your potential. The people who embrace their unique personalities are the ones who turn out to be the happiest and most successful because of the internal harmony they attain.

It's always good to have role models and to strive to become better, but the key is to remain yourself in the pursuit of bettering and enhancing yourself. You can learn to improve your writing style from Edgar Allen Poe without writing *The Raven*. You can learn to improve your painting skills from Picasso without painting *Starry Night*. You can constantly improve by admiring and learning from other people—without *becoming* those people. Grow and improve, but do not change the fundamental nature of who you are for anyone. As my dad says, "Don't do different things, just do things differently." Be yourself and constantly improve, but don't change the true essence of who you are.Along with being able to boost your internal emotional stability, being yourself allows you to block out what people think about you and focus on more important things. By simply being yourself and not following others, you will have a concrete faith in yourself that allows you to ignore what people think of you. You won't care what these people have to say, and your focus will then shift to being happy and successful in life. To dedicate effort to being someone else is simply a waste of your time as it only takes away from your ability to develop the skill of being happy.

Consider venture capitalists, wealthy individuals who invest in small, startup businesses in exchange for an equity stake and/or a royalty stream. Any small business trying to convince a V.C. that they are worth investing in will assuredly be asked, "What's proprietary?" or "Do you have a patent?" or something to that effect. They will look for something that will assure them that they are investing in something that cannot or will not be duplicated. If all companies simply tried to copy all of the products of other companies, they would not get a deal from the venture capitalists. Nobody wants what's already out there. People want something different. With essentially no effort besides deciding and making the choice to be yourself, you can be that person that is different, unique, and admirable in the world. Think of your life as a venture capitalist, except you're investing in yourself. When you have the important factor of exclusivity, you have the first component of being a billion-dollar person!

When you are yourself:
- Your confidence will skyrocket.
- You will believe in yourself.
- You won't be insecure.

- You will trust your own personal decisions.
- People will respect the courage you have to be yourself.

With these types of enormous benefits, you must be wondering, "How can I be sure that I am just being myself? How will all of this be done?" Keep in mind that sometimes, when trying to change, it can be a bit challenging, but with these easy exercises, you will be able to start living life as *yourself.*

Exercises:

1. Start being grateful for your existence and stop comparing yourself to others. So often in life, due to what is depicted on the television screen or magazine cover, we seek to become that which we see. Instead of focusing on being grateful for who you are, it is easy to get caught up in society's norms and be upset that you are not someone else. Strive to become better, but don't forget how great and different you already are and that you don't need to change to become "normal." Every day, simply remind yourself that you are who are and you are absolutely happy with it. It will become easy when you start regularly telling yourself that.

2. Write down 10 things below that you love about yourself. Start each sentence with the phrase "I love myself because . . ." Recite these 10 sentences anytime you feel a loss of identity or you think you are forgetting who you are. Feel no shame! Loving yourself is a major key to happiness. Feel free to go beyond 10 items if you choose. An example of this could be your excellent cooking ability.

1.

2.

3.

4.

5.

6.

7.

8.

9.

10.

3. Write down 10 things that you will ignore/not care about when you are yourself. Start each sentence with "I don't care if/I don't care what . . ." An example of this could be not caring what other people think about you. These exercises will help to instill a love for yourself and allow you to be proud of who you are.

1.

2.

3.

4.

5.

6.

7.

8.

9.

10.

The Best Medicine

Circumstances can cause life to be very difficult at times, as most people know. It can sometimes be a struggle to get through those tough times and create happiness, especially if one cannot find gratitude or positivity in a situation. During these times, laughing, smiling, and finding a burst of hope or joy can go a long way in getting you out of a funk. Both laughing and smiling are greatly beneficial for a happy and healthy body and mind. We can overcome the toughest of sorrows in life by drenching the problem in laughter.

In times of sorrow, most people cannot even think to find laughter. They have the wrong attitude about how to deal with pain. They would rather concentrate on the source of the heartache. Why would anyone want to do this, though? Constantly thinking about the problem and giving it your attention only worsens the situation. If you replace that constant worrying with some laughter, you will be able to kill the pain rather than contribute to its growth. Even if the laughter is only for a short period of time or the smile doesn't last through all of the sorrow, both are still immensely beneficial because they take our attention away from the negative aspect and force us to consider the positive aspect. Scientists confirm that simply faking a smile enhances our ability to think positively.

Psychologists have long stated that looking at something with a humorous attitude allows us to mentally make the problem smaller and puts the situation back in perspective. If we look at all of life with a smile and some laughter, living through circumstantial ups and downs doesn't seem so daunting a task. This is what caused Mark Twain to assert, "The human race has one really effective weapon, and that is laughter." Laughter is truly powerful. Just a little bit can have a dramatic effect on our perception of things and, as a result, positively influence our actions.

The idea that smiling and laughter can get us through anything is best captured by comedic legend Bill Cosby who believed, "Through humor, you can soften some of the worst blows that life delivers. And once you find laughter, no matter how painful your situation might be, you can survive it." This is a very strong statement that is packed with truth: laughter can keep you going through **anything**.

I recognize the concern that sometimes laughing in a tough time can seem inappropriate or even disrespectful.

This is understandable, and if the situation presents itself, such as in the case of death, your best option may be to not laugh. In some cases, feeling the pain directly is a better way of coping with the problem. Nevertheless, laughing, in most situations, is a simple way for you to instantly change your mindset and attitude. Instead of being sorrowful that something didn't go your way, just fake a smile and find something that will make you laugh. If you can't find laughter in the situation itself, go find a person or video or TV show that will make you laugh, and the stress load that your problems place on you will be mitigated.

It is important to know who or what are makes you laugh. If you are in need of laughter, go to one of your known sources of smiles. If you put just a small amount of effort into finding some way to laugh, I assure you that you will find it. Maybe your source of laughter is reading an article or listening to a comedian or playing a game. It is your responsibility to determine what it is so that you know what you can turn to when you are in need of some laughter.

It is also a good idea to try to laugh every single day, whenever possible. It's easy to laugh during the good times, and most likely you won't have to find a specific source of laughter. Laughing and smiling regularly have a tremendous overall impact on your health and hap- piness. They will help you stay positive and keep your mood elevated.

They say that laughter is the best medicine, and all the research behind this claim seems to validate it. Scientists and health researchers have done numerous studies leading to one general conclusion: laughter is an outstanding stress reliever and health booster. So I urge you to try to laugh as much as you can, through both good times and bad. Make laughing as much as you can and whenever you can a priority. You will instantly see a change in the consistency of your happiness, plus be rewarded with excellent health benefits!

Regular laughter strengthens the immune system and eases stress while relaxing the entire body. This means that laughing actually helps combat diseases such as the common cold while giving you a feeling of happiness at the same time. If you are tense or stressed, laughing helps alleviate the pressure you are putting on yourself and restores your good mood. Just think about how you feel after a hearty laugh. Stress disappears with the appropriate amount of humor in your life. Some studies have shown that laughter burns calories and even lowers the blood sugar rate. There is no doubt about it: laughing does the body a lot of good.

The most important thing about regular smiling and laughing is that it keeps us happy and helps us maintain positivity, despite things not going so well. Just a little bit of laughter can go a long away in reducing stress and bringing back a positive mood. In turn, happiness will be created as well.

Exercises:

1. Find the things that make you laugh. Everyone has different taste in terms of what makes them smile and laugh, so it is important that you find what works for you. The best way to do this is to try a variety of things that you think could potentially make you laugh. Consider standup comedy, movies, books, and, of course, people. List the things that make you laugh (or that you think will make you laugh) below, and make this your go-to list for when you are in need of a laugh.

   -
   -
   -
   -
   -
   -
   -
   -
   -
   -

2. Make it a priority to laugh every single day. Write a statement of purpose below stating that you are committed to living life in a more humorous way and that you will laugh more. Write why you will laugh every day and what benefits you seek to attain from your regular laughter. Read this statement every morning.

_____

_____

_____

_____

_____

_____

_____

_____

3. Try to interact with people who laugh regularly. Laughter is contagious, and it's very easy to chuckle when around people who already laugh a lot. My sister Neetu is a good example of this—her laugh is contagious and her nonstop laughter causes my whole family to join in. Below, list some people you know who laugh a lot and vow to start conversing more with these kinds of people.

-
-
-
-
-
-
-
-
-
-
-
-
-

Excel with Enthusiasm

There is simply no way around it—life becomes immeasurably more joyful when you are passionate about it. Whether it's immense love for people, a sports team, your job, or just living in general, life instantly improves upon being truly enthusiastic and passionate about what you are doing. The joy we can attain through simply being grateful in all walks of life and loving all that we have been blessed with cannot be matched.

When you start to love living, happiness will come naturally. However, to love life altogether, you must first find passion in nearly all aspects of life. It will then all come together, and attaining joyfulness will be simple.

Ralph Waldo Emerson declared, "Nothing great was ever achieved without enthusiasm." This is a very bold statement and one that captures the immense importance of leading a life of passion. Eternal happiness, happiness that remains despite life's peaks and valleys, is a great thing. One of the biggest keys to achieving it, however, is having passion in various aspects of life. Even one true love for something valuable brings with it an enhanced level of gratitude and, in turn, a very high level of consistent happiness. That attitude translates to all aspects of life and will help to create a love for life altogether.

If someone is in need of something to elevate their happiness, then they may be in need of a source of enthusiasm. For some people, being grateful can be difficult if they have nothing to immediately be passionate about. So, if this person starts looking for and finding things he or she loves, then the individual now has a passion that makes them happy. If that person pursues the passion with the right attitude, he or she will have a source of enthusiasm that makes them happier and more grateful about life altogether.

The overall importance of enthusiasm cannot be understated. If you don't believe me, consider all of the lessons in this book. As mentioned above, it increases **gratitude** and often also creates a **positive** frame of mind. Having passion makes it easier to pursue and achieve even the loftiest of **goals** (any successful person can attest to this). To a degree, it also helps us to **live in the present** because we are enjoying every moment. **Learning** about something you love is considerably easier as well, and **being yourself** is easier if you love who you are and are enthusiastic about yourself. I could keep on going, but I think you get the point. The bottom line is, to be happy, you absolutely must have some passion.

It is important to realize, though, that passion must be calculated carefully. That is, don't go out and develop a passion for meth or heroin and call that your source of enthusiasm. That is not *positive* enthusiasm, and it is obviously harmful to your overall health. Also, don't make your only source of passion something minor like a sports team that doesn't directly impact your life. As an example, I personally am a huge fan of the Brooklyn Nets basketball team, but that's not the only thing that makes me happy, and it is not my only source of enthusiasm. Things like my goals and my future business plans are bigger for me and more important at the end of the day.

You must keep things in perspective and realize that there is a bigger picture for your life. It is far more valuable to develop a passion for a job or your spouse or a certain lifestyle than it is to have a passion for something that is not directly relevant to your life. However, everything does add up, so try to find positive enthusiasm in everything you possibly can. Most of the time, this isn't an issue if you are willing to find or already know what you love.

I once saw an interview of Steve Jobs where he talked about the importance of doing what you love in life. While discussing the topic, he mentioned several times how successful people have always had a love for what they do. He said, "If you don't love it, you're go-ing to fail." This is because people do not quit on some-thing they truly love. In the same way, happiness comes from loving what you are always doing, which is living. Putting two and two together, it is clear that consistent happiness is composed of a love for everything that life has to offer.

Donald Trump also articulated the idea by saying, "Work really can make you happy, but you have to love what you do." This further reflects the notion that any-thing can make you happy if you love it, and with the right attitude, you can love everything that life has to offer. The important thing to remember is that we have many choices in life. We get to choose the attitude we want to have, which goals we want to pursue, what risks we want to take. If done in a calculated manner, we can essentially live our lives on a basis of things that we love. If you truly want to be happy, it is so important to find things you love—from foods to types of people to activi-ties. If you do this with a positive attitude and an attitude of gratitude, there will immediately be many things that appeal to you. It's all about putting the lessons of this book together to achieve that which you desire.

I love analyzing successful people and seeing how they accomplished such great feats, and it seems that all the greats have always shared this common feature of passion. My father and Aunt Alka are both examples I like to look at; both have had tremendous success in the real estate industry working at OnTrack Realty. When I approach them to learn about what they do, I ask about what keeps them going despite challenging times and struggles. I find that the answer I get with them is true for most successful people in any aspect of life—they love what they do. To them, it's not torture to be working 12, 14, or 16 hours a day, 7 days a week, simply because they have a passion for what they do and they actually love it. Their success can be attributed to the fact that they work so hard and smart and with such enthusiasm that they are able to easily push themselves to keep on working even harder. As a result, they can succeed in their ventures as much as they wish to.

To attain a life of happiness, passion must be found in a variety of aspects in life. I've probably started to bore some of you by consistently repeating this fact, but it's so true! If you love several aspects of your life, you will consistently be happy. Consider how you can love these various aspects of your life more: education, career, social life, health, and spirituality/religion.

Are you embracing the opportunity you have to learn?

Are you doing what you love as a career?

Are you associating only with people whom you love?

Do you love the way you manage your diet and exercise habits?

Do you love your religious/spiritual beliefs?

These are key questions you must ask yourself, and if you find yourself saying no, then you must find out why that is the case and make some changes. If passion is attained in most of these aspects, happiness will be all yours.

Just as Henry David Thoreau, fellow writer and friend of Emerson, once said, "None are so old as those who have outlived enthusiasm." If you have lost your love for life and your enthusiasm for living, then, and only then, are you old. At that point, in that case, you have lost your happiness in life.

Exercises:

1. Fill out the list below with ways you can improve your passion in these aspects of your life. List things you love that pertain to the area, and then see if it is possible to integrate your love with that particular aspect. Whether it's cutting certain people out of your life, pursuing new interests, or committing to prayer on a more regular basis, decide how you will enhance your love in the following fields and write them down.

Career	How you will improve your passion
Education	
Social	
Health	
Spirituality/ Religion	

2. Explore the world in an effort to find what you love. For far too many people, the reason they lack enthusiasm is because of their tendency to not want to try anything new. Go out, explore, and find new things that you love. If you think it is interesting and it is something positive, at least try it. What's the worst that could happen? Start now by making a list of things that you've never tried before that you think may interest you. If you are struggling, get suggestions from people you are close to.

-

-

-

-

-

3. Surround yourself with people you already know to be enthusiastic. Just as with positivity, passion is infectious. Simply by being around people who love life or love what they do, you will start to feel the same way. It will also inspire you to go change what you do to love it or find something new that you love.

Stand for Something

No matter what hand life deals to us, we must always keep believing in order to create and maintain our happiness. This includes believing in our values, ourselves, in our spiritual or religious faith, in our goals, in good fortune, etc. Believing that good will come despite a series of difficult times is part of having a good attitude that will allow you to be happy. It will help in executing many of the lessons taught throughout this book, such as staying positive and being yourself. It will also dynamically change your life by making more things possible for you. Times do get tough, but instead of stressing out and constantly worrying (which only compounds the problem), learn to believe and seek better times. Whether it be faith in your ability to do something or what the future might hold, a simple dose of regular belief will keep you going and help you in reaching prosperity, success, and, of course, happiness.

Belief is essential to being happy for a variety of reasons, the most important, of which, is that nothing can truly be done without it. Strong faith is very important to succeed in anything. Before we are able to effectively engage in any activity, we must first believe in ourselves and our abilities. It makes the task much easier and allows us to expand our horizons in terms of what we are capable of doing.

For many people, life becomes very hectic when the future seems bleak and filled with uncertainty. Proper belief in the good fortune of the future helps to negate those doubts and worries and allows you to carry yourself in a more relaxed manner. Believing that the future will be fruitful is very similar to being a positive thinker, because they both follow a very similar mindset. If you can simply master one of the two, you will possess two skills that will help you quit worrying about the future and start enjoying the present moment more.

Belief is a quality that all successful and happy people must have. It pushes us, motivates us, and allows us to do things that may seem impossible to the rest of the world. Think about J.K. Rowling, author of the immensely popular and successful *Harry Potter* series. Rowling is a true example of going from rags to riches as she fought tremendous adversity in her pursuit to escape from struggles. She was rejected by 12 publishers, but still did not give up and kept on believing. Now she is one of the most successful authors ever, and it is all because she kept working hard and believing despite difficulties. Had she not believed in herself and what the future could bring to her, many of us would have been deprived of her excellent series.

In addition to believing in the future, you should also live by some set of core values. What is important to you and how important is it to you? What things do you think you should be living life based off of? Consider things like honesty, integrity, and responsibility, and how much you treasure these things. How do you feel about making sure these things are adhered to in your life? Whatever values you believe in will control how you live. They will be the basis of many of your decisions, the pillars that hold together the way you lead your life. What you believe in from a moral standpoint will guide you to making proper decisions and allow you to lead a life of more consistency and stability.

These core beliefs should not be sacrificed for anything. Your life should be based on your values, starting with the most important ones according to you. For example, if honesty is most important to you, then in all situations, make sure you abide by that value by making sure you always tell the truth. This, in turn, regardless of the loss or gain, will ensure your happiness as you did not compromise yourself.

After finding what values you really believe in, you must actually practice them in your everyday life. Like the revolutionary Mahatma Gandhi declared, "To believe in something, and not live it, is dishonest." You must find what you believe in and then live your life based off of those beliefs. This will help create a stable identity for yourself and will add more meaning to your life. A life based strongly off of core values has a heightened sense of happiness as well because of the simple fact that immense joy comes with correct beliefs. Knowing that you are leading a good life with balanced and positive values will, of course, cause you to be a happier person.

In addition to believing in a set of values, it is important to have your own personal beliefs and opinions in life. That is, you should have your own opinions on everything in life from politics to sports to education. You should do your own research and believe in what you feel is correct based on your values, rather than following the crowd. This helps you in being yourself and allows you to avoid being brainwashed by what other people have to say on a topic. You must have your own convictions and be able to back them up or you will get stepped on. You can do this very easily by just DECIDING what you believe in and sticking to it. Don't let people tear down your beliefs since ultimately, it is what you believe that matters. Malcolm X voiced this very notion, saying, "If you don't stand for something, you will fall for anything." Rather than allowing yourself to fall for whatever garbage the world has to feed you, choose what you feel is appropriate to believe in and stick to it.

Aside from your basic beliefs to determine how you

live your life, it is also important to believe in other things. First of all, it is important to believe in yourself. Oftentimes in life, all you will have is yourself to believe in; no one else will listen to you, and even your loved ones will think what you want is impossible. The important thing to do, however, is to keep believing in yourself and, if you choose, a Higher Power. No one can say you cannot do something when you believe you can. Your faith in yourself should not be baseless, however. You must continue to work very hard, take risks, and seize opportunities, but at the same time, believe that all you are doing will have an ultimate reward. Goals undergo a significant increase in their power and meaning if they are enforced by a belief that they will be accomplished. If you can maintain this belief in yourself and in everything you are about, you will be able to not only accomplish them, but also surpass all of your goals and be significantly happier. You won't be worried about what other people think and you will be far more ready to excel in life.

You must believe in your ability to accomplish your goals, even when no one else does. Whether it's your goal to be happy, start a business, or expand a company, you must first BELIEVE you can do it before it can actually be done. Oftentimes, the faith itself, if 100 percent strong, is enough to propel you to success and to guide you toward that which you desire. This is called the Law of Attraction.

This law is the idea that like is attracted to like. Therefore, thinking positively yields positive results and thinking negatively yields negative results. If you believe with all of your heart that something is possible, it will be made possible. If you work for it, it will come to you far more easily because the universe will work with you to make it happen. It all starts with faith that it *will* happen, though. It cannot be a halfhearted belief that *maybe* something will happen; it must essentially be a fact. Your belief in yourself and your goals must be so strong that it becomes definite that what you want *will* happen.

Will Smith has often talked about how important it is to believe in yourself and to stay focused. He says to forget plan B because all it does is distract from plan A. You must believe in that which you want, and then stick to it. That should be all that matters to you, and if you believe, the universe will work with you to make it happen. Indian philosophers have long talked about how it is possible to even move mountains with the right attitude, but it does not happen because people do not truly believe that it can happen.

So, from believing in our future to our values to ourselves to a Higher Power, it is immensely important to keep faith through all our pursuits in life. It opens the world to greater possibilities and increases our happiness at the same time.

Exercises:

1. Create a list of beliefs that you value in order to help yourself establish the core pillars of your life. Make sure that the list is arranged in order of importance. Then, next to each individual value, write why it is important to you and how you will make sure to live by that value as best you possibly can.

   ▪

   ▪

   ▪

   ▪

   ▪

   ▪

   ▪

   ▪

2. In order to maintain self-belief and belief in the future, continue to stay as positive as possible and follow the exercises from the chapter on positivity. Also, make sure you have a vision for the future and believe that that vision is possible. In the goals chapter, you already did this and wrote it in the book. Read that statement in a matter-of-fact tone every day so that you can maintain the belief that it is possible and will assuredly happen one day.

Forget the Golden Rule

Growing up as kids, many of us were taught the golden rule—"Treat others how you want to be treated"—and for many parents and teachers, it was the main rule that needed to be honored. However, I feel that the rule needs a bit of an upgrade for it to be properly applied to the idea of becoming consistently happy. This version should be, "Treat yourself well, and then treat others equally well or even better." This new rule states that you must take care of yourself, and then take of others, even better than you would yourself, if possible. I call this the Happiology Rule.

The Happiology Rule, as stated above, is composed of two parts. First, you must take care of yourself. Second, you must treat others equally or even better than you would treat yourself. The whole concept has to do with the notion of becoming happy as a result of doing good and reaping the benefits that come with making others happy. However, before you can do good for others, you must first do good for yourself. Too often, people are unbalanced with their approach in this aspect of life; some people care too much about themselves and forget about other people, and some people care so much about others that they forget about themselves. Both of these are very bad when it comes to maintaining internal peace and consistent happiness.

In order to achieve the ultimate equilibrium in terms of being happy by helping yourself and others, you must first pamper yourself. It may seem selfish, but the only way to maximize how you can help others AND be happy is by taking care of yourself first. You must make sure you are on top of your finances, health, spiritual life, and social/family life before you can help anyone in any of those departments. In other words, practice first, preach second. After you see that you are treating yourself very well in these four aspects, then you can start helping others. With your experience and success in a particular sector, it will become easier for you to help others effectively follow the second part of the Happiology Rule. The four aspects you must concern yourself with are: your finances, your health, your spiritual life (if you choose to follow one), and your social/family life. These four aspects are immensely important in leading a life of happiness and need to be addressed before anything else.

Money or finances can be attained with the practice

of just a few principles from this book. If you are still in school, there is a good chance this doesn't apply to you just yet, but I still recommend reading on. The first factor is making sure you have the right attitude, no matter what job you have. A wrong attitude will yield negative results and cause struggles in your finances as discussed previously. Second of all, you should love what you do. If you don't, either learn to love it or go for something else that you think you are capable of doing with immense passion. Last, set career goals for yourself. Whether it be to get promoted or earn a higher salary, make sure you are always striving for something more. With these three skills, your financial situation will exceed your own expectations.

The next important thing you must do is to look after your health. People nowadays are becoming increasingly unhealthy because of their poor diets and lack of exercise. Major food companies provide people with low-quality, unhealthy foods for the sake of making money. It is important to remember that health is extremely important in your life as it enables you to do many things.

Make sure you are eating healthy with the proper amount of water, fruits, and vegetables in your diet, and a limited amount of oily, sugary, and salty foods. The occasional fast-food meal is fine, but overall, you should maintain a healthy diet. In addition, be sure to exercise on a regular basis. Consult your physician and put together a specific plan for your well-being as far as exercising goes.

Be sure to get an appropriate amount of sleep every night. Oftentimes, when caught up in work or play, it can become rigorous and cause us to go an extended period of time without sleep. Use your time wisely and invest it in a good night's sleep to assure that you will avoid stress and worry and be able to function as an even happier and more productive human being the next day. Avoid drinking excessive alcohol and smoking cigarettes as well, as those obviously become deadly to the body with time.

As far as spiritual and social/family life goes, you must do what is best for you. If you enjoy praying and meditating, reserve time early in the morning for engaging in these practices. Don't get too caught up in your job or money that you forget about your family and friends, either. Set some time out of your schedule to make sure you are spending at least a decent amount of time with them. Being around your loved ones is critical for maintaining happiness.

After you have done these four things and you are comfortable in each aspect, you have completed the first part of the Happiology Rule—treating yourself well. After this, you can move on to treating others even better. This will help you create a balanced execution of the rule in order to greatly enhance your ability to be consistently happy.

I once heard preacher Joel Osteen talk about how God will reward you if you help His children. Whether you believe in God or not, the message is essentially the same: the benefits to you will be tremendous if you are willing to sincerely help others. If you haven't noticed it already, you eventually will—genuinely helping people goes a long way for *you* and *your* happiness. There's a certain joy in life that can only come from knowing that you are making someone else's life better.

As Ralph Waldo Emerson once said, ". . . to know even one life has breathed easier because you have lived. This is to have succeeded." We should make it a goal every day to help someone else out and treat other people better than we would want to be treated. Even the smallest of acts can do wonders for people, and for you.

You might be thinking that you would rather treat people how they treat you instead of treating them the best that you possibly can, but this is not the right attitude to have. A truly happy person must be consistent in this respect in order to maintain their own happiness. If you are constantly changing how you treat others, your own mood will decrease or increase based off of their actions. Stop giving people a reflection of how they treat you and start rising above. Many times, they will rise above as well. I'm not saying to allow people to disrespect you, but do not immediately judge how they treat you and reflect that back. Instead, stay consistent as best you possibly can, and you will be rewarded with happiness.

This is not the easiest thing in the world to do, I will admit. It's very easy for humans to sacrifice a good attitude and good treatment of others when we feel we are being disrespected. The key here is to just keep practicing and making sure you are following the rule. It's not easy, but it's certainly worth the effort. Once you start doing it, you will notice how much happier you become and how consistent your happiness is.

As far as how to do this goes, there are many ways to treat other people exceptionally well. Giving sincere compliments, offering them food or beverages, speaking to them kindly, showing respect, and doing small favors are all minor things that go a long way in making the rule work. It's not necessarily what you do for a person, it's how you do it. If you do it with the right attitude and a mindset of wanting to treat someone well, you will achieve your goal. You don't have to go out of your way to make everyone your best friend, but you should treat everyone, even complete strangers, with the greatest respect that you possibly can. The universe works in a beautiful way; what goes around comes around. It may come from someone else, but it will most certainly come.

There are so many things that you can do to help others and improve the quality of their lives. Most people in the world have struggles that other people will never know about. Something that you do could change their life without you even knowing. Keep this thought process in your mind when you encounter different people in your life. The prominent leader Booker T. Washington once wrote, "Those who are happiest are those who do the most for others." Sincerely care for people and treat others well and you will be happy.

Forget the golden rule and go for levels higher with the Happiology Rule: Treat yourself well, and then treat others equally well or even better.

Exercises:

1. Fill out the chart below. Check off if you are treating yourself well or not for each category. If the answer is no (be honest with yourself), then write in the comment box how you will change. If the answer is yes, write how you could be doing even better. It may be setting more goals, changing your diet, exercising more, or cutting work time, but you should be very specific in your plan of action.

Aspect of life	Treating yourself well	NOT treating yourself well	How you will improve (be specific)
Financial/ Occupational			
Health			
Spiritual			
Social/Family			

2. Make it a priority every day to try your best to treat everyone exceptionally well. Record one person you implemented the Happiology Rule on and how you did it at the end of every day. Do this with more than one person when you are ready until it becomes a regular practice for you. Start recording today by listing some people who you treated exceptionally well and how you treated them well below. Always remember, "You can easily judge the character of a man by how he treats those who can do nothing for him." —Professor James D. Miles.

_____

_____

_____

_____

_____

_____

_____

_____

_____

_____

_____

_____

_____

_____

_____

_____

_____

The Bonus Study:
A Little Extra

In life, when we do anything, a certain amount of something is almost always expected. However, by exceeding that amount and giving more, a new level of happiness is reached for the people on both the giving and receiving ends. Instead of always trying to "just get the job done," push yourself to do just a little more. The results will speak for themselves.

This is a big belief of my father, and I too have adopted it. Why? Because it is 100 percent true. By giving more than expected, we get more. For example, if you work a little past your 8-hour shift at the office, you will be rewarded with more money, greater respect, and a potential promotion. If you study beyond what your teacher assigns you, you will receive superior grades. If you start giving people more than they expect of something positive (kindness, gratitude, etc.), you will be rewarded with a greater sense of happiness. The other people will also be considerably happier.

This principle requires minimal effort and goes a long way in making yourself and others happier. Try to give more than what is expected every single day and the results will attest to my words. You will be happier, and what you gave will come back to you in an even greater amount! Go above and beyond as best you can!

With that being said, I want to leave you with one more gem of Happiology advice: Never get too attached to anything. An addiction to an object or person will always lead to worry, stress, and unhappiness. It is inevitable. If you must be attached to something, make it a goal. Be obsessed with success, and forget all the rest. Like we discussed earlier, goals make you better and happier, but attaching yourself to money, people, or some material object will assuredly lead to a state of unhappiness!

Wishing you Happiology at all moments!

Notes

Notes

Notes

Notes

Notes

Notes

Notes

Notes

Notes

_____
_____
_____
_____
_____
_____
_____
_____
_____
_____
_____
_____
_____
_____
_____
_____
_____
_____
_____
_____
_____
_____
_____
_____
_____
_____
_____

Notes

Notes

Notes

Notes

Notes

Notes

_____
_____
_____
_____
_____
_____
_____
_____
_____
_____
_____
_____
_____
_____
_____
_____
_____
_____
_____
_____
_____
_____
_____
_____
_____